world's greatest grandpa

pops

granddad

papaw

grandpa

gramps

grandfather

granddaddy

world's greatest grandpa

papaw

pops

grandpa

gramps

granddad

To grandfathers who protect
and those who coach;
to grandfathers who listen
and those who tell stories;
to affectionate grandfathers,
and more modest ones;
to all grandfathers and their grandchildren . . .

Concept by Diane Barbara. Design by Diane Barbara and Dominique Beccaria.

Diane Barbara and Dominique Beccaria

Grandfather and Me

Abrams Books for Young Readers

New York

Nowadays, you see all types of grandfathers:
young and old,
big and small,
bearded and shaven,
classic and modern,
grandfathers who wear glasses
and those who ride motorbikes,
hard-working grandfathers
and those who take it easy.

No matter what type he is,
he will always be your grandfather:
your mom or dad's father.
If it weren't for him, you wouldn't be here today.
By sharing this album with him, you will hear the
many interesting things he has to say.

So, grandfathers and grandchildren,
take up your pencils, glue, and scissors,
prick up your ears,
and get ready to talk, share, and
complete this book—this gift—together.

Like a Tree

If his hands feel big and warm when he holds yours . . .

If he often utters the words, "When I was a little boy . . ."
and is slowly losing his hair . . .

If the wrinkles dance across his face when he looks at you and
you grow older and wiser in his company . . .

If, like a tree, he is the root from which your family has sprung,
and you, the child of his child, are a little branch among
bigger ones . . .

Then there's no doubt:
it's your mom or dad's father—your grandfather.

5

Our Family

Every family has a story that goes back far into the past.

To find out more about who your closest ancestors are and how you are related to them, branch upon branch, fill out the family tree on the following page with your grandfather.

In no time, you'll learn a lot about your family.

It's your turn—
check out the tree hidden underneath this page!

Fill in the names, birthdates, and deaths of each of your family members in the little circles above, starting with your own name in the bottom circle.

The History of Our Family

Ask your grandfather to write down everything he knows about the history of your family.
Where is your family from (country, region, city, village)? What is the origin of his or your last names?
Which names have been handed down from generation to generation in your family? Was there ever a famous person in the family?
Or a profession chosen by several family members? Have family members lived long lives?
This will be an opportunity for your grandfather to do some research!

The Memory Trunk

The people and places that make up a family's history yield many memories.
On this page, you can record some of them; for example, a photograph (the original
or a photocopy) of your grandfather's grandparents or his childhood home.
Or maybe even a very old document, such as his great-grandfather's birth certificate!

My Grandfather as a Baby

It may not be easy to imagine your grandfather—who is now much older—as a tiny little baby, crying and sucking from his bottle. Ask your grandfather to tell you everything he knows about his first days of life: when and where was he born (in his home, in a hospital, at a clinic)? How old were his parents when they had him? What kind of baby was he (calm, cranky, temperamental . . .)?

Date: **Place:**

Paste a photo of your grandfather as a baby; if other people appear in the photo, don't forget to identify them! Look closely at how they were dressed.

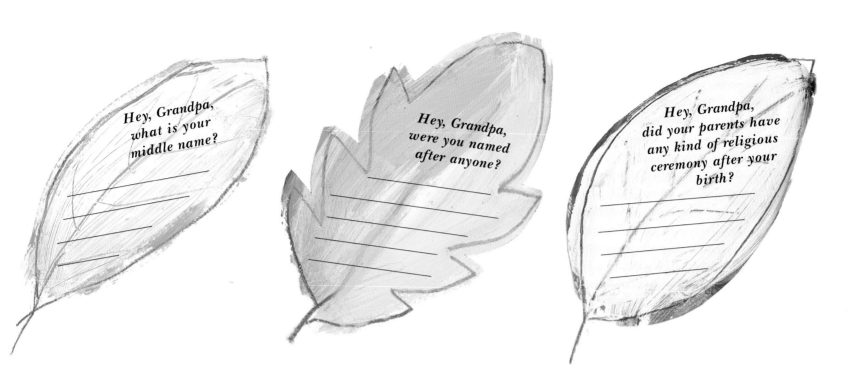

Hey, Grandpa, what is your middle name?

_____
_____
_____
_____

Hey, Grandpa, were you named after anyone?

_____
_____
_____
_____

Hey, Grandpa, did your parents have any kind of religious ceremony after your birth?

_____
_____
_____
_____

**My great-grandparents:
my grandfather's parents**

My grandfather's father   **My grandfather's mother**

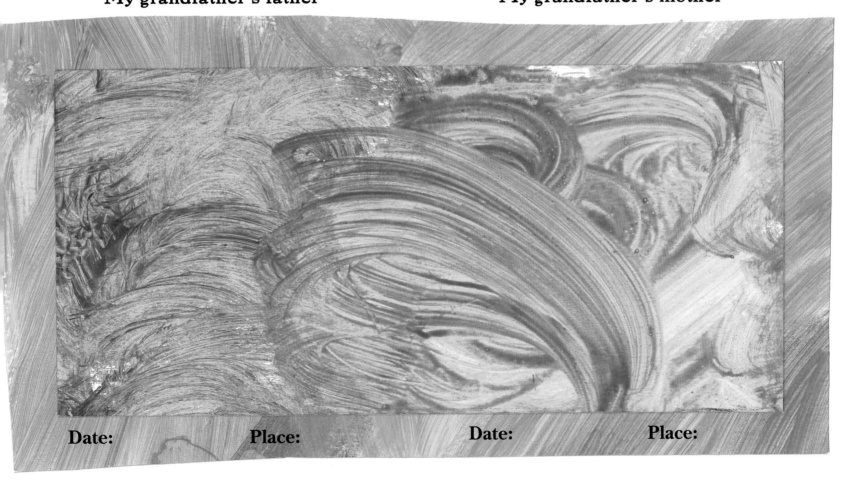

Date: **Place:**   **Date:**   **Place:**

*Paste a photo of each of your great-grandparents, or a photo of their wedding;
then ask your grandfather what he would want you to remember about them.
Do you resemble them? Does your grandfather?*

My Grandfather as a Little Boy

Before your grandfather shares some of his childhood memories with you, take a good look at him. Imagine how he might have looked as an eight-year-old, then sketch it below. How was he dressed? What color was his hair? Was he small and chubby or tall and skinny?

Afterward—and only afterward—paste a photo of him at that age. Does your sketch resemble the photo?

Captured by me!

Captured by the camera!

Date:
Place:

Date:
Place:

His day's activities . . .

When your grandfather was eight years old, he had many
different habits than you. What did he eat for breakfast?
What did he do at night after finishing his homework?
How did he spend his days?

Here is a diagram with nine sections where you can describe
or draw a typical day in the life of your grandfather as a
young boy, showing everything that has changed since his
day!

Tell me, Grandpa!

Family life

Did your parents have a nickname for you?

_____

What kinds of things did you do with your
friends or siblings? _____

_____

And your cousins? _____

_____

What were you not allowed to do? _____

_____

What were you allowed to do? _____

_____

Did you get punished a lot? How? _____

_____

Did you visit your grandparents often? _____

_____

Where did they live? _____

What did you call them? _____

_____

What kinds of things did you do with your
grandfather? _____

_____

Hey, Grandpa,
were you given
an allowance?
How much?

_____

_____

Vacation and free time

What were your best friends' names? _____

_____

What games did you like best? _____

_____

Did you have any after-school activities? _____

_____

Where did you spend your vacation? _____

_____

Who did you go with? _____

_____

What kinds of things did you do on vacation?

_____

_____

Hey, Grandpa,
did you practice a religion?
If so, which one?

_____

Hey, Grandpa,
where was your
favorite hangout?

_____
_____
_____

Hey, Grandpa,
what did you like to do
when you were alone?

_____
_____

Hey, Grandpa,
did you have a girlfriend?
If so, what was her name?

_____
_____

Secrets and little things

How did you like to dress? _____

_____

What did you like to eat? _____

_____

What did you hate to eat? _____

_____

What kind of candy did you eat? _____

What did your bedroom look like? _____

_____

What was your favorite song or story? _____

_____

What was your most precious toy? _____

_____

What is your favorite childhood memory? ____

_____

_____

And your least favorite? _____

_____

My Grandfather at School

Once upon a time, on a sunny fall day, there was a little boy who left for school carrying a big leather schoolbag, his pockets full of marbles and chestnuts. It was the first day of school, and he wondered what the other boys in his class would be like. At that time, boys and girls didn't share a classroom. Tucked away in his schoolbag were his books covered in paper, a folded apron, a small chalkboard, an eraser, chalk, a fountain pen, and some blotting paper, in case of mistakes!

Look closely at these pages with your grandfather and point out the differences between his classroom and yours.

His life as a schoolboy

Hey, Grandpa, did you like school? Why or why not?

_____?

_____

Hey, Grandpa, what did you do on the weekends?

_____

_____

Hey, Grandpa, what didn't you like about school?

_____

_____

Hey, Grandpa, where and what did you eat for lunch?

_____

_____

_____

Hey, Grandpa, what is your favorite memory from recess?

_____

_____

Date: **Place:**

Paste a photo of your grandfather's classroom in the space above (you can photocopy it and reduce the size to fit), or a photo of him as a schoolboy, or even a page from one of his notebooks.

And as a jokester . . .

Grandfathers also know how to have fun; ask yours how
he goofed around when he was little, with friends or
family, around the house, on vacation, or at school.
Have him to tell you all the dumb things he used to do,
including the dumbest!

_____

_____

_____

_____

_____

_____

_____

_____

Only your grandfather can fill out this page!

My Grandfather as a Teenager

Some grandfathers turned fifteen in 1930, and others in 1960. Between those years wars were fought, followed by great economic expansion, resulting in a completely new world. But regardless of his present age, your grandfather was once a teenager, a time when his voice changed, he experienced the horror of pimples and his first facial hair, and he wanted to stay out late and felt the need to rebel.

Though people back then didn't talk as much about teenagers as we do now, your grandfather certainly has some memories from his teenage years to share with you.

Date: **Place:**

Paste a photo of your grandfather around the age of 14–16.

Military Service

Some grandfathers were in the military when they were younger. For many of them, this marked a major turning point in their lives: they left home for the first time to experience a different, and often difficult, way of life. They were taught to obey, cut their hair very short, and spent their time learning how to defend their country.

In words . . .

Where did you do your military service? Can you show me on a map? _____

_____

How long did your military service last? Were you able to come home once in a while? _____

_____

What exactly was your mission? _____

_____

What did you learn during this period of your life? _____

_____

Did you get your driver's license during your service? If so, tell me about it . . .

_____

_____

Did you have any specific chores? If so, what were they? _____

_____

Do you still see any of the friends you made in the military?_____

_____

And in pictures!

Date: **Place:**

Find a photo of your grandfather in his military uniform and paste it above, or draw a picture based on his description of the uniform.

My Grandparents' Wedding

Grandfathers are usually not as reliable as grandmothers for recalling details of their wedding day. But asking the right questions is the best way to obtain the information you seek. Here's your chance to find out more!

Look for photos of your grandfather's wedding and paste them here; then, using arrows and captions, describe the events of that day (the location, the witnesses, bridesmaids and groomsmen, weather, reception, flowers . . .). The more captions and arrows you have, the better the investigation!

Hey, Grandpa, how did you and Grandma meet?

_____

_____

_____

Hey, Grandpa, did you give Grandma an engagement ring? If so, what did it look like?

_____

_____

_____

My Grandfather as a Father

If you find it hard to believe that the person you call Grandpa was once a young father, paste a photo of him with his children (your dad or your mom, and your uncles and aunts . . .) and look!

What kind of dad did he look like?
Affectionate? Strict? Worried?
Distant? Playful?

Date:
Place:

My grandfather looked like the kind of dad who

_____

_____

Tell me what my dad or mom was like!

What kind of kid was my dad or mom? _____

How about my aunts and uncles (my dad or mom's siblings)—what were they like? _____
_____

Did you have a nickname for my dad or mom? If so, what was it? _____
_____

Were you strict? If so, how? _____

What did you not allow your children to do? _____
_____

What was the dumbest thing my dad or mom ever did? _____
_____

What was his or her worst punishment? _____

Did you play with your kids? If so, what did you do? _____
_____

What was my dad or mom's favorite toy? _____

What did you enjoy doing with him or her? _____

What kinds of things did you teach your kids? _____

What is your most precious memory of him or her? _____
_____

And the worst? _____

Do I resemble him or her? If so, how? _____
_____

My Grandfather and Work

The workplace has changed a lot since your grandfather started working. Vacations may have been shorter than they are now, and the hours of the workday were different. Ask your grandfather to talk about his profession to better understand the working conditions of that time.

His profession: _____

_____

_____

_____

_____

_____

_____

_____

_____

_____

_____

_____

Hey, Grandpa, when you were little, did you know what you wanted to be when you grew up?

Hey, Grandpa, did you take special classes to help prepare you for your profession? If so, what were they?

_____

_____

Hey, Grandpa, what was your first job and how much money did you earn?

_____

_____

Hey, Grandpa, what qualities did you need to succeed in your profession?

_____

_____

Hey, Grandpa, what has changed the most in your field since you started working?

_____

_____

Hey, Grandpa, how many hours a day do you (or did you) work?

_____

Hey, Grandpa, what do you appreciate the most (or did you appreciate the most) in your career?

_____

_____

The road to retirement

Nowadays, people tend to retire in their sixties. Some choose to continue working beyond that age, and others decide to stop everything and relax. Still others take advantage of this time to do things they've always dreamed of, such as traveling, planting a garden, or even taking care of their grandchildren!

There are also people who decide to retire before the age of sixty. But regardless of when they take it, retirement marks a very important turning point. What does your grandfather think about it?

My Grandfather and Me

When you're lucky enough to have a grandfather, you feel it practically from day one: the day you were born. On that day, your grandfather became a grandfather either for the first time, or once again. Between the two of you, only he can remember your first encounter!

Our first encounter

_____

_____

_____

_____

_____

_____

_____

_____

_____

_____

_____

Hey, Grandpa, how did you first hear about my birth?

_____

_____

Hey, Grandpa, what is our age difference?

_____

Every age of our lives

Find some photos with your grandfather in which the two of you appear together—
alone or with other family members—and in which you are seen at various ages of life.
Which of you grew faster?

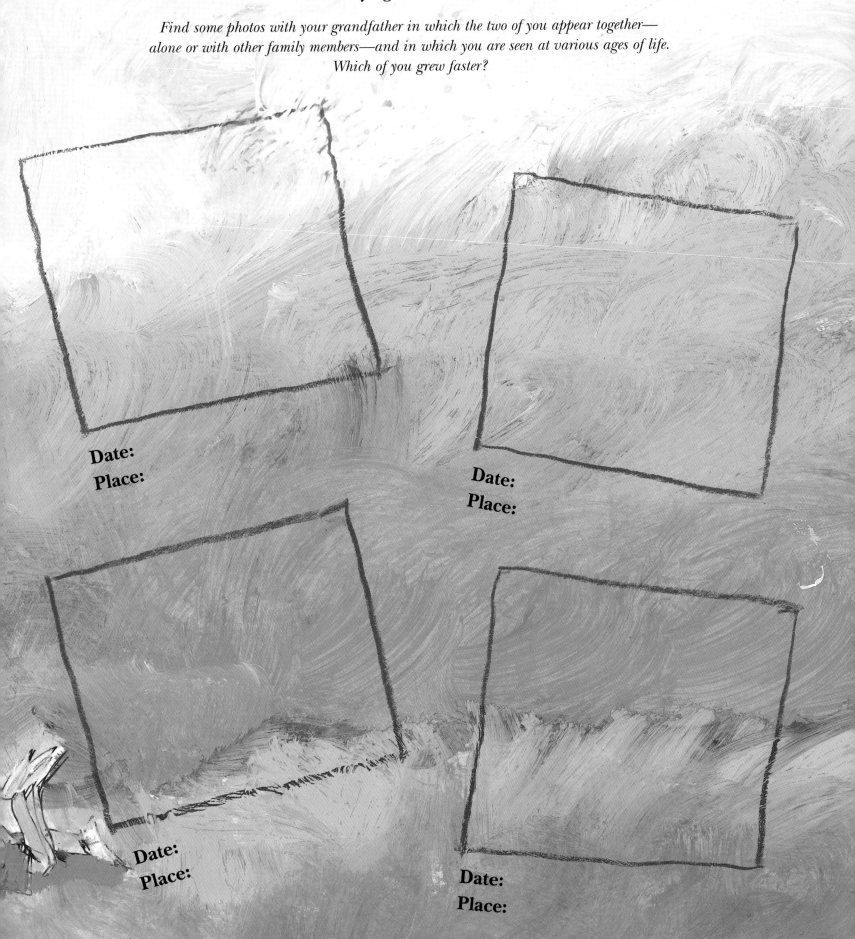

Date:
Place:

Date:
Place:

Date:
Place:

Date:
Place:

Why I Love Him

We all have different reasons for
appreciating our grandfathers. Some
of the reasons are written on the
stones in these two pages. Now think
of some other reasons and write them
on the empty stones.

Pretend that all these stones were
placed here so you can tell your
grandfather the reasons why you love him.

Later, when you read this page again, you
will undoubtedly think of other reasons . . .

Because he's fun to play with.

Because he takes my
father's place when he
can't be there.

Because he is
big and strong!

Because, in my eyes, he's
Santa Claus: He always has
a gift, a magic trick, or a
secret to share.

Because he always laughs at my jokes!

And why do you love me, Grandpa?

Because if I get a bad grade, he reminds me that I can do better next time.

Because he teaches me new things.

31

How I See Him

How well do you know your grandfather: his face, clothes, tastes, personality, and habits?

Here are some tests to quiz your knowledge!

I can see Grandpa with my eyes closed

Close your eyes. Have your grandfather ask you the following nine questions and fill in your answers in the first column. You will earn one point for every correct answer and zero points for every wrong one. If you score less than three points, try again later in the second column, with your family's help!

What color are your grandfather's eyes? _____

What color is his hair? _____

Does he have a mustache or a beard? _____

Does he have a big Adam's apple? _____

Does he wear eyeglasses or a hearing aid? _____
_____

Does he wear cologne? If so, what does it smell like? _____
_____

How is he dressed today? _____
_____

Does he wear a watch? If so, what does it look like? _____
_____

Does he wear any jewelry? If so, what? _____
_____

Total

Questions about his tastes and personality

To test how well you know your grandfather's personality,
try to finish the following sentences.
Then ask your grandfather to finish each sentence.
Compare your results!

My grandfather loves to . . .

My grandfather can't stand . . .

His best friend is . . .

His favorite kind of music is . . .

His favorite food is . . .

My grandfather's dream is . . .

His favorite TV show is . . .

When my grandfather
is angry, he . . .

The thing that makes him
laugh the most is . . .

According to me   According to Grandpa

Grandpa's pockets

Try to guess what kinds of objects your grandfather carries in his pockets, and then write or draw the ones you didn't know. Your grandmother can help you!

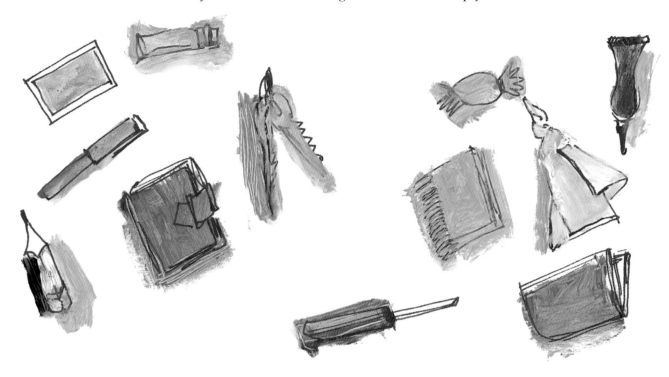

Photo of my grandfather's house, room, furniture, or favorite object

Date: **Place:**

Grandpa, from head to foot!

In the box below, sketch your grandfather exactly as you see him.
Don't forget details about his belongings: a hat he sometimes wears, his glasses, suspenders, etc.
Your own children will appreciate this drawing some day!

Grandpa's age : _____

My Grandfather, the Accomplice

Children often say that a grandfather is like an elderly father. We discover life with him (without getting punished!). He's also the best accomplice. Becoming an accomplice isn't easy, however. Certain rules have to be respected!

Secret greetings

True accomplices always have a personal way of greeting each other:
a secret handshake, a password, a facial expression.
Invent one with your grandfather, and either sketch or write it on a piece of paper;
then fold it in half (so no one can see what it says) and tape it below.

Pact of Brotherhood

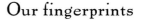

Our signatures   Our fingerprints

Being accomplices also means staying together from this day forward.
To seal this promise, you can choose to sign a contract, exchange a handshake,
or record your signatures and fingerprints on this pact of brotherhood.

Exchanging good ideas

Now that you're accomplices, it's time to give each other some pointers . . .

Me

You'll teach me about an activity you like, such as: _____

_____

You'll entrust me with one of your things:

_____

_____

_____

I'll tell you the game I'd most like to play with you: _____

_____

_____

My Grandfather

I'll teach you to play a sport I used to love, such as: _____

_____

I'll give you a special belonging of mine:

_____

_____

_____

I'll tell you the game I'd most like to play with you: _____

_____

_____

To Us, Grandpa!

Rules

– 1 –

Two players: you and your grandfather

– 2 –

Form a jury of at least two other people with the help
of your grandmother, brothers and sisters, and cousins.

– 3 –

Ten tests will be administered
in one day, one week, or one year.

– 4 –

100 points wins a secret prize to be determined by the jury.
After each test, the player who wins will earn 10 points.
In the case of a tie, each player will win 5 points.

– 5 –

You may substitute two of the tests with two others
invented either by the players themselves or by the jury,
provided that they are chosen unanimously.

– 6 –

It is strictly forbidden to cheat.

– 7 –

It is also forbidden to
allow lazy grandfathers or
cranky grandchildren to win.

Test list

1

Play the game:
Play a round of your newest video game.

2

Trip to the store:
Head to the grocery store as fast as you can and buy three items off Grandma's grocery list, for example: sliced bread, three tomatoes, and a bouquet of flowers. Don't forget the change!

3

To the kitchen!
Make your favorite recipe. Let the jury taste it!

4

2 plus 2 equals:
Do your multiplication tables (or, for younger kids, addition tables) without making any mistakes.

5

Roll your marbles.
Start with 5 marbles each. The first person must place his marble 10 feet away. The second person has to try and tap it with his own marble. The person who hits the most marbles with their 5 wins!

6

Memory!
Place 10 objects on a tray, memorize them, then cover them with a cloth and try to name everything that was underneath.

7

1, 2, 3, sink!
Skip a stone and try to make it bounce three times. The bathtub is off-limits!

8

The forbidden word:
Decide on a "forbidden word" with your grandfather. Then tell a story about a particular subject for three minutes, without uttering the "forbidden word." For example, talk about your last vacation on the beach without using the word beach.

9

On your mark!
Bike or run around your house as quickly as possible. The jury will record your speed.

10

A good shelter.
Build yourself a cool fort. Boxes are allowed.

The Merry-go-round of Life

Each line in your grandfather's face, every crease of his hand, tells a story, if we take the time to read them.

For some, life is like a merry-go-round. When asked "Is ten years a long time?" they respond, "Not at all!"

For others, life is better savored slowly, and ten years seems like forever!

What does your grandfather think? Write his response— and your own ideas—here.

My Grandfather and History

Grandfathers often have a unique perspective—gained from a lifetime of experience and reflection—when they talk to us about events that happened forty or more years ago in the United States or elsewhere in the world.

No matter his age, your grandfather has lived through some very important events. He may even have participated in them. Ask him to tell you about an important historic event from his life.

_____

_____

_____

_____

_____

_____

_____

_____

_____

_____

Record your grandfather talking and, if possible, write a little summary of what he told you.
You will be happy to read it again in the future!
Don't forget a title!

Grandpa's word!

It's a well-known fact that all grandfathers have at least one story that they love to tell over and over again, especially during family gatherings. Hearing it for the thousandth time may make your eyes roll.

Here's a place reserved especially for your grandfather's story—a story you can keep forever.

_____

_____

_____

_____

_____

_____

_____

_____

Grandpa's pride

During his lifetime, your grandfather may have received a prize, a medal, a trophy, a diploma,
or some other kind of distinction. Paste a photo or a copy of one of his distinctions in the box below.
If he's truly a champion, make a list of all of his accomplishments!

My Grandfather's Wisdom . . .

Your grandfather has lived through some life-changing moments, such as marriage, becoming a father, working, losing a loved one, making life-long friends, traveling, voting, working, etc.

Each individual experience taught him a thing or two. Now, here's your opportunity to learn from his many life lessons.

Tell me, Grandpa!

What is your greatest wish for me in life? _____

_____

_____

What must I do to be a good grandmother or grandfather? _____

_____

_____

Which quality of yours helped you the most in life? _____

_____

_____

Do you believe in God? _____

_____

_____

Briefly explain some of your political ideals to me: _____

_____

_____

Tell me which book you'd like me to read, either now or later in life: _____

_____

. . . for the Future

I, too, could be a grandmother or grandfather some day!

What will I say about my
grandfather to my own
grandchildren?

_____

_____

_____

What would I like them to
call me?

_____

_____

What is the first thing I will
teach my grandchildren?

_____

_____

_____

*Ask your grandfather to
make a sketch of how he
imagines you'll look later
in life, much later . . .*

Age: _____

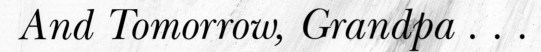

And Tomorrow, Grandpa . . .

You and your grandfather have just exchanged the most precious of gifts.
You devoted your time and attention to him, and he did the same to you.
Now, you have your very own book to protect, reread, and keep forever.

Underneath this album lies another gift.
A hidden gift. A profound gift.
This gift is called strength.
It resembles a little stone that each of you can hold in your hand.
It says:

> I know you better now,
> I understand what I mean to you,
> And this gives me strength for tomorrow.

Table of Contents

This book was created by

_____ and _____

on _____

Production Manager : Alexis Mentor

Library of Congress Cataloging-in-Publication Data
has been applied for.

Printed and bound in Belgium
10 9 8 7 6 5 4 3 2 1

HNA
harry n. abrams, inc.
a subsidiary of La Martinière Groupe

115 West 18th Street
New York, NY 10011
www.hnabooks.com

granddad

gramps

grandpa

world's greatest
grandpa

pops

papaw

grandfather

granddaddy

grandpa

gramps

papaw

granddad

world's greates
grandpa

grandfather